# School Days

Shelley Rotner & Sheila M. Kelly
Photographs by Shelley Rotner

Millbrook Press / Minneapolis

# When we go to school . . .

We walk.

We take the bus.

We ride.

The teacher greets us at the door.

4

I put my things
in my cubby.

We meet on
the rug to
plan the day.

We check our jobs.

I mark the calendar.

I show the weather.

# We learn new things.

I'm learning how to write letters and sound them out.

Reading is hard for me, but my teacher helps.

I like math patterns.

I love science!

I like to count.

# Sometimes we have free time.
## We pick what we like to do.

Puzzles are
my favorite.

I like to build
with blocks.

I choose the sand table.

We love to play with puppets.

# We line up to go to special classes.

It's fun to be the line leader.

# Some days, we go to the library.

I check out a book.

I find my favorite book.

# Other days we go to art.

I love to paint!

We like to draw.

In music, we play instruments and sing songs.

We love to sing!

# At gym, we play games and sports.

# It's lunchtime!

I bring my lunch.

I get lunch at school.

We eat with our friends.

# At recess, we get to play.

I'm happy when I see
my big sister.

# Some days, things don't go right.

One day my feelings were hurt, but my teacher helped me.

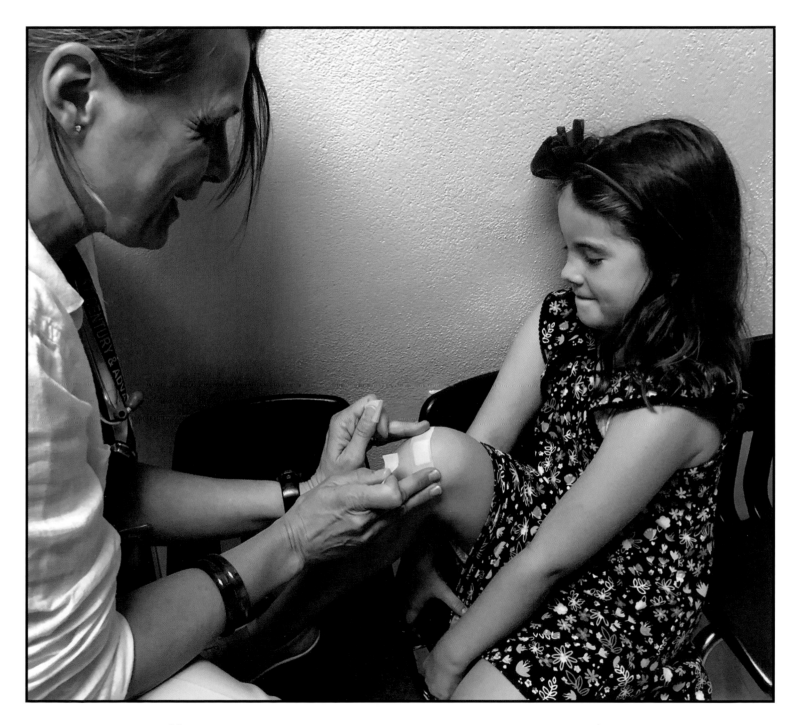

When I fell down, I went to the nurse. She took care of me.

# Every school is different.

My school has a garden.

We take turns picking and watering.

# Some schools have animals.

Our class has a bunny!

I love to hold the guinea pig.

# On special days, we take field trips.

We went to the zoo.

I held a baby lamb at a farm!

The science museum had
a dinosaur skeleton!

We saw jellyfish at
the aquarium.

At the fire station, I got to sit in the fire truck!

# Every day is different.

We learn new things and make new friends.

What do you do at school?

In memory of my dear friend Sheila Kelly.

She was my confidante, collaborator, and coauthor. Thank you for being there in words and wisdom— intersecting, connecting, creating, and sharing magical moments—over all those years. —S.R.

Millbrook Press™
An imprint of Lerner Publishing Group, Inc.
241 First Avenue North
Minneapolis, MN 55401 USA

For reading levels and more information, look up this title at www.lernerbooks.com.

Designed by Kimberly Morales.
Main body text set in Billy Infant. Typeface provided by SparkyType.

**Library of Congress Cataloging-in-Publication Data**

Names: Rotner, Shelley, author, illustrator. | Kelly, Sheila M., author. | Millbrook Press.
Title: School days / Shelley Rotner & Sheila M. Kelly.
Description: Minneapolis : Millbrook Press, 2020. | Audience: Ages 4–8 years | Audience: Grades K–1 | Summary: "There's a lot to do at school! Bright photos of a wide range of young kids and simple text offer young readers a look what happens throughout the school year" —Provided by publisher.
Identifiers: LCCN 2019051380 (print) | LCCN 2019051381 (ebook) | ISBN 9781541557765 (Library Binding) | ISBN 9781728415703 (Paperback) | ISBN 9781728401485 (eBook)
Subjects: LCSH: Schools—Juvenile literature. | Teachers—Juvenile literature. | Learning—Juvenile literature. | Arithmetic—Juvenile literature. | Reading—Juvenile literature. | Play—Juvenile literature. | Libraries—Juvenile literature. | Art—Juvenile literature. | Singing—Juvenile literature. | Group games—Juvenile literature. | Physical fitness—Juvenile literature. | Day—Juvenile literature. | Education, Elementary—Activity programs. | Classroom learning centers. | Group work in education.
Classification: LCC LB1513 .R68 2020  (print) | LCC LB1513  (ebook) | DDC 372—dc23

LC record available at https://lccn.loc.gov/2019051380
LC ebook record available at https://lccn.loc.gov/2019051381

Manufactured in the United States of America
1-46170-46162-1/21/2020